My seven Book

by Jane Belk Moncure
illustrated by Linda Hohag
and Dan Spoden

Library of Congress Cataloging in Publication Data

Moncure, Jane Belk.
 My seven book.

(my number books)

 Summary: Little seven introduces the concept of
"seven" by interacting with seven of a variety
of things, some of which are grouped and regrouped to
demonstrate adding and subtracting.
 1. Seven (The number)—Juvenile literature.
[1. Seven (The number) 2. Number concept.   3. Counting]
I. Title.   II My seven book.   III. Series: Moncure,
Jane Belk.   My number books.
A141.3.M672 1986   513'.2 [E]   86-2594
ISBN 0-89565-318-4 -1995 Edition

My seven Book

This is Little seven .

Little seven lives in the house of seven.

It has seven rooms. Count them.

Every day Little seven goes for a walk.

One day he walks in the rain.

He sees one
big duck . . .

and six little
ducks
in a pond.

How many all together?

Some ducks say, "Quack, quack, quack."

Some ducks dive under the water.
They are looking for snails.

Can you count how many heads
and how many tails?

Next Little  seven sees frogs on a log.

He counts five ...

and two more.

How many all together?

Little  claps seven claps. Can you?

How many frogs dive into the water?
How many frogs stay on the log?

Little  walks past the pond. He comes . . .

to a big rock.

He sees a mama turtle and lots of
little turtles. Count them.

Little  finds a net.

He catches the . . .

little turtles. How many?
How many turtles are left?

The little turtles are sad. So Little  lets three go. Then he lets three more go home to Mama.

Now count the happy turtles.

Next, Little  seven sees a big mound of sticks.
"I will sit and rest," he says.

But a beaver peeks his head out.
"You are sitting on my house," he says.

Little  jumps away. Out come

two big beavers . . .

and five little beavers. How many beavers in the whole family?

"Watch us play," they say.

Little  says, "I will play too."

He hops seven hops. Can you?
Guess what he finds.

He finds a big sandbox with a toy train in it.

How many cars is the engine pulling?

Little  builds a track for the train.

Then he makes a tunnel.

"I will pull the seven cars through the tunnel," he says.

Little pulls and pulls.
Three cars come out.

How many cars stay inside the tunnel?

Little seven pulls some more.

How many cars are through the tunnel now?

How many cars are still inside?

Little  pulls again. Does the whole train come through the tunnel?

"It is getting late. I must go home. I wish I could come here every day of the week," says Little  .

Little  counts the days of the week —
Sunday, Monday, Tuesday,
Wednesday, Thursday,

Friday, Saturday. Can you? How many days all together?

As he hops away, Little  seven sees

some money in the road.

Little  picks up a nickel and two pennies.

How much money all together?

Little  seven hops to a

candy store.

CANDY

He looks in the window.
He sees lots of lollipops.

A sign says:  lollipops 1¢ each.

"Whee!" says Little
"I can buy lots of
lollipops. I have seven cents."
How many lollipops can he buy?

He buys three cherry lollipops
and four grape lollipops.
Count them.

Little 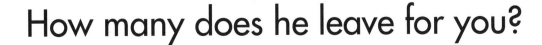 eats two lollipops.

How many does he leave for you?

Let's add with Little  .

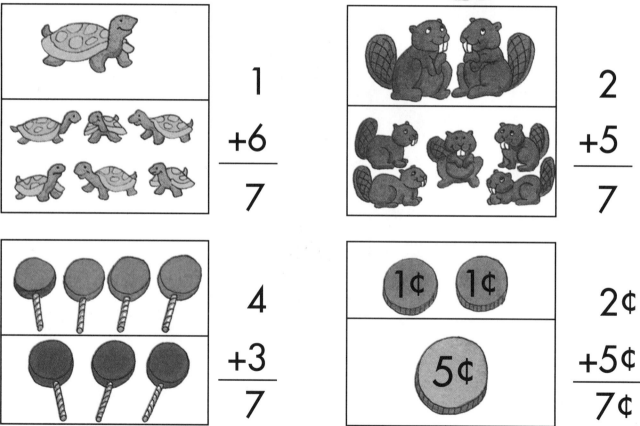

$$\begin{array}{r} 1 \\ +6 \\ \hline 7 \end{array}$$

$$\begin{array}{r} 2 \\ +5 \\ \hline 7 \end{array}$$

$$\begin{array}{r} 4 \\ +3 \\ \hline 7 \end{array}$$

$$\begin{array}{r} 2¢ \\ +5¢ \\ \hline 7¢ \end{array}$$

Now you find more ways.

Let's take away with Little  seven.

$$7 - 3 = 4$$

$$7 - 2 = 5$$

$$7 - 4 = 3$$

$$7¢ - 5¢ = 2¢$$

Now you find more ways.

Little seven can make a 7. Here's how:

He can make the word seven. Here's how:

seven

You can make them in the air with your finger.